I Got
to Know
Nature

Thank you for
being FANTASTIC!

a collection by
Christine Weimer

Book II

ISBN: 978-1-7354874-6-5 (Paperback)
      978-1-7354874-4-1 (E-book)

Edited By:
Christine Weimer

Cover Design and Formatted By:
Lindsay Tisi

Author Photography:
Elmer Quintero

Second printing edition 2020

www.ourgalaxypublishing.com

OUR GALAXY
PUBLISHING

to the strong-minded Taurus woman who has remained a
constant in my life for as long as it has ever mattered: Lindsay.

thank you for always knowing my nature better than me and
for never allowing me to forget all the worthy parts of this life.

this collection is because of you..

the only way out, is in

Matriarch

let's take a shot
for the matriarch
who taught us
the greatest power
of a woman
is she can do
what a man can do
with chains
at her feet
a knife
in her back
and a baby
on her hip.

Introduction

It happened after the dust settled. I was a Tainted Lionheart, overlooking a kingdom I had not yet built for myself but was all mine for the taking. Fresh paths and another unknown journey greeted me. At first, I did not know how to move. Where did I want to go now that I rose from the ashes? Who did I want to be after fostering enough ferocity to breathe fresh air into my new freedom? What would I take with me?

For some time, I was afraid to sit with myself. By this, I mean heeding to the calling that my heart was giving me when it was time to look deep inside—to understand what was underneath. Sitting with myself meant paying attention to the silence of my solace, getting used to the idea of listening to what my mind was trying to tell me without all the noise.

It scared me to do it because I feared what I'd hear. I feared I would find out I was doing it wrong. I feared having to admit some things I never wanted to convey. I feared having to take accountability for my role in a setback. I feared reeling through memories I had long tried to bury, only to end up with the same unpleasantries.

Except stagnancy would have crumbled me faster. I realized that rather quickly. So, I took a risk like the lioness I have vowed to myself to be, and I ran bare through every territory of myself I didn't want to cross. I got to know myself.

I reflected on the person I was before, though I did not become her again. I reeled through recounts of the places I've been, knowing I could never go there again. I presented myself with the retellings of the things I'd take with me into the after, knowing I had learned so much. And it was all rough stuff. It was mind-bending and strength-straining. Getting to know my nature as a human, as a lover, as a woman, was the most challenging work I've done. It was also the most important.

I am forever evolving. There are always parts of myself I will have to reassess. Thankfully, there will always be things to hold on to. There will always be a foundation for my nature when I am dedicated to the knowing.

But the journey does not end here. The journey never ends, really. Not even when my soul ceases to occupy the body Mother Nature has blessed me to rent for a while. There's a price to pay for renting this shell, though. And it's worth it even when I'm bruising, even when I'm digging deep through the toughest parts of my inner journey. There is abundance on an alternative path that I am claiming.

Something is stirring on that path. There is matter intensifying on unknown roads I have yet to discover, but I know I am getting closer to uncovering it. That cosmic creation I yearn for myself is waiting as I get to know my nature.

Or rather, let my nature get to know the new me.

Christine

part one:

The Nature
of a Human

I Got to Know Nature

I got to know nature barefooted.
running through trees that trickled twigs
sharp enough to puncture through the very ground
that promised me a steady path,
yet gave me no gravity to sink my feet into
and no gavel to beg for some order
from the gravel I was sliding over.

I got to know nature bare-chested.
wind lashing with force to tug at my bones
as leaves came smashing into my eyes,
already half-blind
from the dust that whirled around
as I tried to make my way through weeds
that mocked my meek body as it swayed unpredictably.

I got to know nature bare-handed.
grasping stones between thorns
to throw at the sounds I did not recognize
amongst the hasty rain
melodiously hitting bare arms
that flung themselves about
hoping to feel something
that's more like a dancing daffodil
and less like a dreaded drenching storm.

I got to know nature with a bare soul
and a bare spirit,
and the fullest desire to let it take me
as far as my body would go
before scarred skin and manic minds
would bring me to my knees
in surrender to the forces
I have fought to succumb to for miles now.

I got to know nature purging through its elements
in an essential need to prove I could keep fighting.
provoking paths and prying productions
of its rudiments rattle through pieces of me
that are trying not to tear what remains
because nature can be so cruel to the kind.

I got to know nature when I learned
that its jarring gestures would never falter
to foster my fears in its foundation,
but that I could foster my ferocity
through its very core into me.

feeding fires, and swallowing storms,
and inhaling the wind
while I dug its dirt to match the path
I wanted for myself.

I got to know nature
when I embodied its components
because I realized that the only way out
was in.

personifying nature.
encapsulating its energy.
seeking what is free.

Keep My Mouth Shut

choke on my words to spare wrath of yours
legs shaking, nail-biting to the core
swallow my skin until it bleeds
hoping it'll keep what I wish to say at bay
deep down in my throat

stuck in my windpipe
there is an urge wanting to purge
from my mouth
but I don't want to clean up the mess

spit hits my face as you keep rambling
scrambling for a point
that will never be there to make
suck down all the air in this room
because maybe if I pass out
I won't lash out at you

eat my lips so they won't sink this ship
while I am struggling to get to shore
without causing any more damage

ravage all things I've tried to establish
your slander slithering its way out to sea
it can't hurt me
while I am consumed
by chewing myself down
so you can't

I refuse to engage with you
and gosh, the rage that would come through
fighting through actions I can't undo
if only you knew

Misfits

hell is a place where our guilt lives
misfits of misunderstandings
wandering in wrongdoings
coping with culpability
in a way that ignites flames
we just can't seem to put out,
can we?

guilt is an underworld of self-condemnation
regrets and repentance
damning our dishonor
swimming with shame
in a way that roughens the tides
we just can't seem to coast with ease,
can we?

self-condemnation is an abyss of misery
calling for contrition
drudging through delinquency
shaking the sins in a way
that still leaves debris
we just can't seem to clear away,
can we?

hell through humiliation
mingling with mortification
groveling with guilt

eternally damned.

Hiding from Shadow

I tiptoe around my shadow
so as not to wake it.
I need no more darkness in day.

I have felt my way through unlit rooms
and exhumed myself without my silhouette
to dim me.

my shadow has blocked the sun from hitting me,
and now I run through hickory
without its overcast to follow.

I let my shadow rest under the earth I stand on
so that anywhere I turn, I am unconcerned
with the darker parts of me.

but there's always irony.

you see, blackened beds play tricks
on heads that rest on them,
and I cannot sleep with the light on.

my shadow lays dormant in the day,
but at night, I am near fear
over the way it greets me overhead.

casting shadows linger above eyes
that cannot escape it.

not in the darkness.

I tiptoe around my shadow,
but only for as long as the sun stays awake.

I cannot hide from my outline when the moon calls.

I fall under penumbra that shows what I keep buried
in opaque casts that last until day breaks once more.

I made a choice to shove my shadow
where it cannot be seen in light,
but I bear the burden of its brooding nightly..

Fire and Sorrow

I reign over fire and sorrow—
those who melt under me seek spark
from my sadness
to lay it onto their kingdom of rage.

they all want a piece of debris—
floating through fountains of fears
causing flames that erupt villages of vexing,
restless spirits.

forests forage for flight—
knowing their roots are implanted
where their leaves burn
and branches snap as seas seize
to hold their water,
drying.

misery feeds this fiery family—
of the misfit lands discovered ages ago,
when sadness sashayed sarcastically
into a sanctuary that used to be full of serenity
and is now a sick scene of self-sabotaging.

but they flock despite the drought—
for a fragment of suffering
and an infinite inferno that keeps them stuck
between torching and troubling themselves
through tribulations that torture
their tomorrows.

they know not what they do—
they do all they think they know,
blazing with the melancholy
that is me.

they all want a piece.

Life Left

I have never watched life leave the room.
I have been collecting fears of death
since birth,
but I have never looked it in the face.

until echoing screams brought on nightmares
from the dreams of a woman trying to trap life
in a room where it was begging
to escape.

but I couldn't keep it close.
prayers and shrieks pranced around the room
in effort to contain death for revival.

but there is no way to jar up life.
I had to let it go.
had to watch life leave,
the most unpleasant scene I have set my sights on.

death has an ugly way of greeting its match
when it's come to take life away.
it spares no remorse
as it drains breaths of love from life
not ready to leave.

but no one is ready to leave.
and I did not want to let go.

no choice to be had,
no grasp strong enough,
no bellows to beg life not to go.
it is gone.

no doors or windows slammed shut
could keep it from its exit.
death does not reason with the living.
it just helps it leave the room
lifeless.

Death Draws a Crowd

death draws a crowd
that may only be seen by the living.
it attracts somber faces that mask curiosity
"how did it happen?"
you listen for whispers from the living
who wonder how death got here.

death is marked with a praise
as if accomplished something grand
"their pain is over now"
but for the living,
it has only just begun.

death draws crowds of the living
who gather to watch grief grow in the shadows,
not knowing what to say.
extending apologies and sprinkling peonies
on a grave that gave a new home
for death to live.

it draws a crowd of dead things
as life clings to what has left us.
arranged in rows for those alive to mourn.
born to die yet we try to avoid what we know
must come to us all.

death calls and draws us in,
though we have been one of the multitudes
who join in on the sidelines,
"I don't want that to be me"
but while death draws a crowd of the living, it is lingering.
creeping and slithering through what is alive,
even after it just took life away.

death lurks until it inserts its sights
into the next of the crowd
whose doors it will plow through,
and one day it will be you.
"is your pain over now?"

Changing the Story

I change narratives with additives that suit the way I can cope best with how things go. I'll admit that. I manipulate my fate in fear I can't facilitate my feelings. I hate to sit with myself. So, my head becomes a stereo to sanctimonious scenarios that place me as the martyr while everyone's a monster in this story that I won't find glory in.

I take inventory of wrong-doings and misusing done upon me. I use it as my weapon to let out my aggression because circling around deception is simpler than granting myself the confessions I need to take accountability for. I control the whole situation by flipping the script, thinking I'm equipped to change something I did not write myself.

It's all because I'm scared. I'll admit that. I hate to accept what I cannot change. I rearrange things in my head to create a spread I can somehow live with. But with one swift kick into solitude, I'd face my place in the middle of the mess.

I repress the notions that open the doors to facing the truth of the matter. Refusing to clear out the chatter of my scattered conclusions. Developing illusions while refusing to see things as they are. Coming so far without really dealing. Pushing away from the truth of my
healing, which is to look in the eyes of the prize I didn't win.

I'm working on it. I'll admit that. Perfecting the art of accepting what is. Directing my feelings within. Not putting a spin on why things ended as they did. Forbidding to outbid the ones who took a pen to that paper with me. I see that I can't erase what others wrote. No cause for misquotes. Allowing myself to sit and recommit to only what will benefit me.

I haven't always done that.
I'll admit that.

Shattering Patterns

I follow patterns I know do not serve me. I go back to the same things I am used to because familiarity was never fearful to me. But lately, it is. Lately, I have been afraid of what is always the same.

I choose roads I know lead to dead ends, and I force myself to go back down them with a new outlook each time, thinking they will be different. I have learned that no matter how many times I walk down the same path looking for a fresh face, I will only be greeted by those who have always been here before.

Who and what is here does not serve me anymore. It ignites a sense of worry within me because manic minds can be made in the mundane. My spirit is seeking connection to something that will help it grow, but I've run out of space in this place I keep walking through while looking for a way to expand.

I can't stand the excuses I make for staying in this box. I've convoluted fairytales for why keeping things the same will save me. I know they won't. What I've grown accustomed to is not the same as who I want to become.

I need to tear apart the designs I've devised for so many nights. Dead-ends did not lead me to control the mosaic made outside the confines I've restricted myself to. I am limiting myself to small-scale shapes, knowing I am meant to be embellished through triumphant trails that do not lead me in the same direction I have identified as the only one I could walk.

Plain patterns of paths I have photographically memorized cannot define my nature any longer.

Today, I am seeking a novel way to adorn a fresh composition. It is within me to innovate new intuition. Letting go of a limiting ambition to remain the same, aspiring to claim clarity in my complexion.

Creating new patterns. Old stigmas—shattered.

Bad Guy

I am not one who likes to hit below the belt. Power trips attached to reckless words do not ignite a spark in me. No head high when I have to be the bad guy, and I do not get my rocks off from throwing stones at people.

I know my house is made of glass, and that is why I am cautious of where I shoot my ammo. Pulling the trigger on a low blow is not my MO, and I've never been one to run my mouth with no place for it to go.

That's why you need to know I never intended to present this side of me. There's just only so much I can take before I break out with claws after pulling at straws trying to understand why you thought I deserved what you gave me. Betray me, blame me, then try to defame me, and expect me not to come at you knowing this is how you repay me?

I think we've both learned a lesson here about trusting other people. I guess sometimes the most doting ones are still the most deceitful. And I'm not the woman who likes to stick a dagger wherever she can, but it wasn't my plan to draw defense from this intense offense you tried to slash through my chest. So, don't tell me I don't have a right to be angry. You crossed a line, and quite frankly, making this right is impossible. I'm past that now.

Let's skip to the part where you take accountability for dropping bombs inside my head and disrupting my tranquility. Because though I'm not one who likes to hit below the belt, there's no planet where I could let you get away without me first having my say about the traitor's hand you've dealt..

But I know actions speak louder than words. I've said my peace, and I know I have been heard. Tail between your legs, covered up so no one else can see except me, but that's okay, really.

You and I know the truth of what happened here. Harsh words and insults only scratch the surface. But I'll repurpose this mess so I can destress and focus on my success. I'll move on with this as remnants of a bygone phenomenon that no longer dominates my headspace.

I won't erase you. You'll straggle through my brain, but you won't cause pain anymore. That's the beauty of knowing your limits, trusting your gut, and adjusting what you choose to inhibit. I did it. Prohibited your energy from occupying me. And you can falsify me. Modify the narrative until you falter in your alternate reality. I don't care who you make me out to be. I'm aware of my role. The rest is history. Why you did what you did—left a mystery.

My, the simplicity of a life lived with full authenticity—no duplicity of intent to keep me from moving on. Going strong without the thread you strung along.

I don't get a head high from being the bad guy. Can't be the antihero for the crimes you need to rectify but won't. Walking away is how I'll justify the way you dissatisfy with the chaos you've provoked. Won't utter your name from my throat.

Revolt. Reproached. Revoked.

Table

I have eaten alone enough times to know I'm okay with empty chairs. My table is big, and I have been known to create feasts from the fruits that got me where I am as I sit here writing this.

I am the woman whose chairs are often filled with bellies I keep rounded on the back I labor in the field with. I pick the bounty that rests itself upon the table where you engorge yourself.

I serve you with the diligence of my efforts and spoon-feed you only the finest of every ounce of my hard work. Your chair will be warm, and you will never be thirsty with the fountain I have gone through depths to build for you to drink from.

I am the woman who knows how to create everything from the nothing you have brought to the table I allow you to spill your wine on. I guess the silver platter I have rested in front of you has glared too bright for you to see how good I am at cleaning up messes while I work, though--whistling.

I am the woman who can serve, and sweep, and shine your fucking shoes on the way out the door. Rest assured, I am also the woman who knows damn well when her crops have been eaten by crows masked as pheasants who do not give thought to the damage they might cause to a harvest as precious as mine.

Sit around my table, but do not steal from me what I have not presented to you. Share my reaping with me as I give it to you, but do not help yourself to the pickings I have plucked and piled with the hand you are biting. How silly of you to think that though I am all-work so you can all play that I am also a dull woman too.

It takes a light too luminous for your weakened eyes to fill this table, and your presence amongst it does not keep my bounty from flowing.

I have eaten alone enough times to know I'm okay with empty chairs.

And I will whistle while I work. Sweeping. Shooting the birds.

Clapback

I never claimed to know it all, but I've learned enough to say that tearing up my home won't make yours look less in disarray. You try to infiltrate the haven I create, yet somehow the grass still looks way greener over here. You've got a lot to learn, my dear.

I almost want to cusp that mocked-up face of yours in pity of such petty ways, but I've learned enough to know fake things will tarnish, and I'm not about to have anyone's stained-up sham on my conscience.

I don't really give a damn about your counterfeit kindness and your quite frank forgery because that's your own journey. But don't you dare think you can blink your eyes and pervade your parade of parasitic ways around the walls I have layered with hands that have favored a fortress, while yours have fabricated a portrait that will fade as soon as the sunlight torches it.

Bolted barricades are not needed to fight your demons from my domain. It is sanctioned in sage, rooted with authentic auras that shield and wield against the battlefield you keep trying to manifest here.

Let me make this clear.

This home is not yours to corrupt, and I don't mean to be abrupt in my bluntly confronting this little emotional spill you seem to be having because I am not one to judge this grudge you're grabbing at.

Still, I haven't even begun to tell you how offended I am that you even tried me.

Now, I won't waste my breath breaking all that down to you. Describe it as I'm just not vibing with it, though we know it goes deeper than that, and I'm not really sure where you're at in terms of what you wish to accomplish. I can just promise you will only demolish whatever you have left that hasn't been taken by your own theft to become this great pretender, a contender to your own personal presidential potential in a race that literally nobody is running for.

And let me say to a degree, I want to give you some humanity. I cannot imagine how you keep up with all that deceiving. Lord knows I'd be grieving with guilt if I ever built my life on such phony things. That kind of exploiting has got to keep you up at night, but I'm not here to make this right for you.

Maybe if you didn't cross me the way you did, this would be a different story since I've got compassion overflowing and know all about collectively growing. But there are many ways for us to have had a disagreement, and instead, you tried to intervene in my most prized achievements, and there's nothing that I ever did to deserve that mistreatment.

You're going to have to go your way for the last time now. There's only so much I'll allow of you to try to take that's mine somehow.

I never claimed to know it all, but I've learned enough to say that choosing me as your prey would never go your way, and this house will be a home no matter who you try to betray.

And that display of greenery you keep on saying is designed by the sublime sunshine with those so-called cleansing crops you've seemingly been offering...

I know enough to say they could use a little watering.

part two

The Nature
of a Lover

Mercury Memories

memories made in mercury.
taste of metal meddles in my mouth.
we were transcending.
minds mingled as we surpassed Heavens,
enchanting eclipses while we crystalized together.
red hues danced while we heated
the elements between us.

two states became one in these skies.
planets aligned under the precise personas
we presented
as we expressed ourselves
through intimacy exchanged
as the matter rearranged
between us.

memories made in mercury
quicksilver into decay.
bursting and disbursing,
hovering over the surface.
separately waiting
to be swallowed by the stars.

Autumn Drunk

I have been drunk on autumn wine,
staggering with calming drink in hand.
liquor-lipped with forced laughs
under a lustful moon.

there is a certain elegance
of death in the air
as brazen desires consume my wrath,
wishing it would let peace intervene.

but crops of peace have been cut
and rotted to their silent roots
while I bathe my thoughts
with this inverted heart
that longs to be made of herbs and sleep,
drifting under doting trees.

Speechless

I have been the one with too much to say
for far too long.
now, I'm speechless.
voicebox ripped by choice,
and I've stripped myself
of the lips that loved lasting lengths
of conversation it could have with you.
they're sealed shut now.

my diaphragm has been crushed
by a falsified trust residing in the gut
that thought it was right about you.
but it wasn't.
I ripped out my lungs
tired of speaking in tongues
to a shell of a soul that used to control
my emotions.

oceans of commotion in my mind
streamlined to nowhere.
I will not let them be uttered.
keeping my words down in the gutters
where I was left.

I used to have plenty to say.
but today, I chose silence.
defying what I used to speak about.
I'm bowing out.

Self-healing

do not expect closure
from those who ripped open your flesh.

the attacker will never be the healer.
learn to stitch yourself.

Holding the Sun

I was holding onto the sun for us.
drifting through winters
just to find some warmth for dormant bodies
restless from too long a lonely sleep.

you knew I was hoping for the heat
to rise between us.
it was you who turned up the furnace
in the first place.

racing without pacing ourselves
through all we felt burning up for us.
aware of what would happen
when fires erupted
because our bodies almost set the bed on fire
on that very first night.

you chose to freeze me out
instead of continuing to feed my flames
and I cannot imagine
why cold over comfort
was the option you set out for us
after all that fuss over flames igniting,
sparks flying, desiring to drown
as we melted our frozen hearts
between those frosty, faint souls of ours.

did you find a new fire to foster?
a more homely nature
than the glacier I was trying to break down for you?
I stopped holding the sun.
the sky is much darker
and I know I'll be back asleep soon.
And I know I'll be back to sleep soon.
dormant and lonely,
resting coldly without you.

Alliterated Damage

dancing dangerously within dungeons of diluted delusion,
denouncing derogatory dustings under duress.
dress drenched in definitive diligence,
discerning detrimental discords
that drown in dysfunction.

distinct disappointment directs
to the distance, drifting.
dismissal dominates the drama
while discretion is discovered.
diving into dynamic,
despising the distortion we dragged,
disgracing the discussion that divided
our drunken dreams.
detaching with discipline
and delighted determination,

dancing dangerously within dungeons of diluted delusions.
dozen dragons don't discourage my duty
to dash through doors,
devoted to developing the deepness
of divine I deserve.

daring to declare dynamite days.
devising. designing. doing. done.

Fences

I build fences around the things I need to protect. I nail boards together twice my height, so even the tallest men can't see over this yard. For years, it was a dumping ground of toxic waste, a place for men to leave scraps amongst the rubbish of those who loitered and littered there before.

I build fences for no trespassers to cross, but I carved a spot just for you to come and go. I don't know why, though. Maybe it was the way you saw me as the garden to which I've bordered this wood around, or perhaps it was because the space got a bit lighter the moment I shaped that door for you to enter. It could have been the way you tended to unseen flowers that rarely got sun before I let you over this fence or the way this fence did not seem needed once you were there to care.

I build fences just to tear them down for you, and it's true I had no idea what I was getting into.

I just knew for once this yard was not a discard pile and that some men could be fences too.

But fear does funny things when you are used to jaded junkyards and twisted trash bins. I constructed gates but never cleaned up the mess of lovers' past, and I did not know what to make of a cleansed yard used to clutter, that had no barrier to hide from anymore.

I build fences to tear them down only to rebuild them once again, and this time I did not engrave a place for you to enter. I stand in the center of this space I am boarded into, and I can't remember why emptying yesterday's decay seemed scarier than starting over with you today.

I chose to stay locked away with all that lingers here, and it is much dimmer without you.

I build fences only to try and sneak a peek over its length because there is light in the distance, and for a second, I think it could be yours. I jump to try and catch a glimpse of you glowing through gardens and radiating the ruins you restore with that gleam of yours.

Yet, I could not steal a stare.

Darkness pours over the outdoors I am trapped within as I build more fences so that even the day won't reach me. Maybe that'll teach me to toss aside lasting lusters that made their way over tall fences without an ounce of destruction.

Regrets of emotions I misconstrue are all that seem to break through me now. I keep building fences around this yard I need to protect, wishing I could still connect with you.

A Story Lives Here

Loneliness is a hollow home with pins dropping like hail as the coffee pours. Loud. Everything is loud in the nothing of clanking pins, and trickling caffeine, and a woman whose breath hisses under dinging and splatters of all the deafening nothings that make up a haunted house.

Loneliness is shuffled feet across creaking floorboards because loneliness is built within old homes that have not been tended to in quite some time. Teetered knees crack with each humdrum move of a woman whose eyes do not break from their daze into the nothingness of everything she cannot be unseen in deluded hallways constructed by ghosts of a full home now empty.

But a story lives here, still.

Timber tales are told through windowpanes nailed shut because loneliness does not let the light in. A woman gazes into planked glass panels as shaky hands scratch ruffled hair that stays unclean because pipes will rattle once the water's on, and ears will pop when rumbles and clanks squeal through concrete walls that long to scream the truth of how loneliness got here in the first place.

Sips of coffee turn to gulps of heat blazing down the throat that has been burning since growling ghosts set this lonely house on fire. Aflame. Ashes of a voice once used lay amongst the dust that has now settled within the frame of boasting beams that know very well what it entraps here.

Listen for shushed mouths and shrieking silence, and you will hear the recount of how rugs got pulled out from under a meek body that shattered into pieces on that very rotted floor. Catch the whoosh of the rug as it smacks on top of scattered fragments of a woman's remains, and you'll swear you hear the cries as it crashes down.

Loneliness is an explosion of echoes and an overload of ominous narratives that blare on repeat as they rustle through knocked-down doors and tore up cabinetry.

Loneliness is a woman who's stuck inside a haunted house, consumed with pockets of possibility that are sealed and tucked far from a lonely woman's reach.

Loneliness is a purgatory.
Purgatory is a haunted house.
A haunted house is a woman.

And a story lives here.
Still.

Dancing in Cemeteries

I kept you in the purgatory I created for us.
your body left long ago,
but I've trapped the remnants of your spirit
inside the narrative I've made up in my mind.
you are a ghost here,
and I am caught between worlds,
spinning a tale of delusional scales
where I didn't fail, and you
are not a phantom.

I planted some daisies for you.
they say new life grows on graves,
and I am hoping you'll push your way up again.
you buried yourself with the shovel,
and I dance on the dirt where hurt converts
to assertive conjuring of the world
where we are conquering our wildest dreams together.

my lace, your leather,
untethered yet intertwined in a bind
that would carry us even through
the darkest of limbos.
but our fantasy bit the dust on its way
six feet down deep.

and I creep around your tombstone
prone to the fallacy that's got the best of me.
I'm stuck here trying to pull you into this world.
desperation unfurled as I curl in a ball
trying to stall our inevitable truth with my screams.

dreams rip from the seams of the dress
I've made a mess of.
scratching and clawing while you're withdrawing
lower below the surface of a purpose
only one of us claimed

I aimed too high to let you die out,
yet it's a copout for you to linger here.
pointing a finger at the wrong villain of this story.
(that would be me.)
but if this is my allegory
then you're a manifestation of my fears.
and it's been years of me holding on to dead things.

weighting myself because deflating myself in flaws
awards me more applause
than living in my truth does.
flaws are putrefied omissions
where conditions of truth cannot take root
because we all need to persecute someone.

don't you see?

I keep decay around me
knowing how profoundly I need to live again.
but I'm stuck in the shadows
trying not to impose on this decomposing body
housing a rotting spirit.

let's play dead together,
just us two,
making do with fire and brimstone
we can call our home.

torments of hell on a carousel.

is this what infinity looks like?

December 10th

Sliding your fingers around the same places you always used to explore. Roadmaps you remember in a snap. One tap, and I am strapped around every inch of you that overlaps mine. There is a bassline playing to our steady swaying, a low sequence in tune to high frequency. Obscenely rich in perfect pitch. Spellbinding while we're finding each other again.

And it didn't take much. But we were never lost, were we? Just buried under shame and fear, steering clear of a reckoning that always comes to nightly sinners. Yet, I still feel like the winner here. You're near ecstasy, and all that was perplexing me drowns under our rhythm because that is how our system works. You smirk, knowing there's euphoria in my hands. All the plans that we made cascade down our skin as we begin to sing songs of hope. Cutting the tight rope we've had to walk on for far too long. Stringing along with new ties that comprise all that we fantasized about.

Sliding your fingers around the same places you always used to explore, leading to my lips with my hair wrapped in your fist. Pulling. I always follow your lead, pleading for more, feeling so sure of how pure the future looks for us now. But I am not one to confuse sensuality, and your fingers that were sliding are now gliding down my throat. I choke, and you rip my voice box with one single grip. I am stripped of the speech you know can shout and shriek this from the rooftops. You're burying us again, aren't you?

So, it's true. Our love can only exist in the dark. This spark preserved to be observed under a cold moon before it makes its way back underneath in the sun. I am still shocked by the way you took my words from me, knowing I could see it all so clearly, while you slid your fingers where heat lingers and tides guide where waves will crash at their highest peak. But we don't speak about that in the day, isn't that right, dear? I am not baby girl in the light, and you will fight just to sanctify a reputation that hasn't been worthy of salvation since the moment those fingers slid over mine for the very first time

Sliding your fingers around the same places you always used to explore. What more did you really need? Doesn't greed concede at some point? Roadmaps you remember in a snap, leading to lips with my hair wrapped in your fist. Was there more that I missed? You kissed the sweet spots and rocked back and forth to the rhythm only you and I could make. But how much more could I take?

Sliding your fingers around places you cannot explore anymore. I don't belong a nightwalker. Sweet talker in my ear while I slowly disappear like the puppeteer I feared I'd always been. But I will free myself of the wickedness you've become infamous at pinning me as the villainess for.

Sliding your fingers around places you cannot explore anymore. Slamming your hands in the door just to even the score.

part three:

The Nature of a Woman

A Mother's Cry

I am riddled with remorse when my daughter sees me dragging feet in last night's clothing while I pour my third cup of coffee before 10 AM. I want her to value the start of each morning, but sometimes I just want to stay in bed all day. Instead, I force myself to dress and make her blueberry pancakes while I pick at dry cereal because my stomach hurts when I'm in this place, but I don't want my daughter to think that breakfast isn't the most important meal of the day.

Sometimes, I swim in selfish sins on days I don't want to put the work in because I want my daughter to be proud to work hard. I wish to run from obligations and avoid communications, but I will not let her see me lagging. So, I pull out my journal and place pen in hand because my daughter needs to know that her mother follows her dreams consistently.

My mother always told me a clean home was a happy one, so when I trip over toys and slip on sock monkeys on my way to dishes piled in the sink, I grasp onto the guilt that greets me on the way to the floor. There are days I could take to tunnel vision of the tornado that seems to have hit this house, but if I do, she may not know a happy home. So, instead, I internally curse my way through back bending and dust demolishing with a smile while my daughter makes a mess behind me cheerfully.

On days I wish to cut the sunlight out and wallow in my worries, somehow it is shining its brightest, and I know every child needs their dose of boasting sunbeams. So, I follow my daughter dancing daintily outside while trying not to drowse into the dirt below my feet because my daughter will know the importance of free play.

There are nights I could crash into my couch and turn off that ticking clock in a blink, but bubble baths and bedtime stories are part of our routine, and my daughter needs to end her day with clean hands and a mind full of wonder.

I wonder if she will ever know that without her, I might sleep the day away and never enjoy the sunshine because nighttime can't come quick enough when you don't want to put the work in, and I don't have much of an appetite, anyway. But I mark mascara on these tired eyes, flatten out my wrinkled shirt, and run through fields with my daughter, whose laugh produces sparks of light in me.

Rosy cheeks induce contentment in my spirit, and her joy jolts life within this heavy heart of mine. Her sense of wonder makes my dreaded daily duties wisp away in the wind. Moments creating memories with my daughter make me forget there are ever days I just want to stay in bed all day because I know I wake for her.

I will always wake for her.

Survey Says

I have been measured by body. Survey says I was half decent—for a fat chick. Could have scored better if I had more cake to back me up, but overall, would recommend to that single guy they think is pretty cool, but women don't really go for because they say he's too nice--or ugly. They can't remember which one.

I have been measured by style. Studies show that shift dresses do nothing for a big girl's figure, and I'm crazy to cover up the only assets that I have. May have done well with a low-cut shirt instead, but floral-print suits me enough to make me seemingly approachable.

I have been measured by nature. The polls show I curse too much for a lady, and my voice tends to be a bit too loud when I think I have something important to say. But they say any woman can be tuned out when needed, so generally, it doesn't pose an issue to my report.

I have given a fresh look to that report after years of living life based on its ratings, dating the so-called nice guy, who was never really nice, and trying to show cleavage where I could, and most times, I kept my opinions to myself.

Now, I sit with societal tallies that don't mention much of my character. They forgot to write down my loyalties, and I see no word of my resilience. I flip through pages of my analysis, and I see nothing that speaks of my knowledge. No one documented the places I have had to go at far too young an age and the people whose mistakes I had to learn from—rising above it all.

I see something about my apparent lower-middle class, but where is the part where I'm credited for always working for more than what was given to me? I'm ripping these sheets to shreds, and still, the parts about my heart are hidden.

I think it's time I wreak havoc on this system because I have a few things to say about the ones who designed the very method that's had me convinced I didn't measure up.

Their time is up on dictating how I should be viewed because no one should have the right to decide that but me. I want to be ruled by how I pour my spirit into those I love and how often I try to be better than I was the day before. I want the world to know me for the way I project my light onto it and not the way my curves look in that light.

Strip me bare of this shell, and still, you will see a woman who should be surveyed by her strength, not her structure.

Measure my soul, or do not try to see me at all..

Bloom Over You

you layer petals on top of your chest,
believing there is weight in numbers.
if there is anything for you to bury yourself in,
it may as well be the most delicate of nature's beauty.

lungs tighten under lily leaves piled with peonies,
and the heart starts to freeze
as baby's-breath blossoms
sink solemn scenes deeper
into your diaphragm.

but while you are denting soil
trying to cause turmoil to your destiny,
you do not see the seeds shifting
under the very substance that is you.
creating root from your resolute grounds,
spreading through dirt across bounds
you had not expected
your intrinsic spirit could go.

and like so, you lay thinking you'd have succumb
to the heaviness of hibiscus
and hyacinth
until you faded to fertilize the daisies
that push their way back up from below

except despite it all,
what you saw as a pitfall
was your instinctual need to interweave souls with soil
to create power in both sun and wallflower.

a suppressed metamorphosis made permanence
for marigolds to bloom in cold,
and morning glories reign under the moon,
a commune of calla lilies and carnations
bloom over your very foundation.

you have generated new life
from dead things.
everlasting springs splurge to saturate
all that you create
while you thought you'd be
withered with wisteria by now.

yet some way,
you've turned catastrophe into a bouquet,
proving you are meant to survive
for those who long to be alive
within greenhouses you've contrived,
and these flowers will thrive on your earth.
scents of sage engage the sanctity
of your rebirth.

now do you see all you are worth?

Wise Women

wise women keep their mouth shut.
they don't hum songs of agony
where others may hear their tune
because no one wants to sing to the rhythm of blues
when they are already dancing in yellow.

wise women smile while walking miles
with secrets on their backs
because no one wants to see sad faces around here—
chin up, lady.

wise women act like ladies
who shake their heads politely
because they are slightly less threatening that way.

wise women bury memories with kerosene
while they light their cigarette
because if the past combusts,
then no one can live to tell its story.

wise women live lies
because it's easier to be blind in silence
than it is to be too forthcoming.

wise women know their honesty
would condemn too many souls
because when true stories are told
there is a ripple effect.

wise women know better
than to cause a ripple effect
because the last domino will always fall on her.
crushing wise women with the weight of the world.
unfurled yet whirled around by a design
contrived in social ties we won't let break us.

wise women do not break.
they bend and adapt
to the inapt souls they're cursed with.
going to church with all they cannot say.

but maybe someday...

Things for Her to Know

I need you to know I will hurt you.
I will act on impulse and yell too loud,
and sometimes,
I won't understand you at all.

I will disappoint you.
I will sometimes let you down,
and there's a chance I will make promises
and there's a chance I will make promises
I cannot keep.

there will be days I do not show up for you
the way I should.
sometimes, I will act selfishly,
and there may come a time when I will be blind
to all the things I should've seen coming.

I may not always wear the face of a woman
you are proud of,
and some days, you may not like me at all.

but I need you to know that I will always try.
I need you to know
for every day you feel ignored
is every night I lie awake pining
over how I could make your life better.

when I do not fit your vision,
rest assured I do not look
with pleasured eyes in my mirror.

in moments you do not feel connected to me,
know there are days
where I am not connected with myself.

but we are always connected.
you and I are made of tiny particles
merged in ways too strong
for the boldest boulders to break.

I need you to know
I will do you no harm with deliberate intent.
I will never leave you.

I will always save my brightest days for you.
you are my brightest day.

Bridges

I had no intentions of watching
this bridge go down
but it is falling,
crumbling to remnants
as it hits the river underneath.

I know I started the fire.
I never claimed to be a fair lady.

it was the friction
of my frustration and fears
rubbing together through woods
I've never seen before
that somehow set a small patch aflame.
a surface fire started
as I tried to climb uphill
to see over the forest's summit.

as doubt creaked,
sparks caught speed,
and I was scared of what I didn't know
would be my solace.

embers with amber hues and baby blues
took over greenery with its glow,
and I paused at the peak of this mountain
when explosions erupted behind me.

the whoosh of the water wafted wind in my way.
I did not flinch.
I did not fumble back,
and I did not faint at the sight.
because I would not have ended up
at the top of these terrains
had I not been tainted
by what taunted me
on the other side of that bridge.

I turned my festering failures into flames
as I crossed an unfamiliar overpass.
foreign felt better than false.

the fire that burns the path
to where I no longer want to go
is all I needed as I move forward uphill
with the flames that help me see
all I had to do was let go.

turning to tomorrow.
blazing towards the sun.
igniting new incandescence.
building new bridges to cross.

Suit & Tie

they will tell you
your body
is a threat
to men whose ties
have been wrapped around their necks
a little too tight.

your waist loosens the cuffs
on the wrists
of their collared shirts
and belt buckles
are known to get unfastened
by the mere look of a woman
who dares to wear a low-cut shirt
around here.

they will tell you
the miracle
to which your body can create life
is a threat
to men who have trouble understanding
you can do something
far more powerful
than them.

threatened men
are known to use their freshly-tailored suits
to cover you
from being seen in this world.

do not let them.

your body
is not to be caged
or molded
into boxes that fit the design
of a threatened man's
patent leather shoes
that love to walk
all over the backs that bend
in efforts to expand the womb
that carries their very being.

threatened men
think they can rip us
from what keeps us in control
of the very humanity
of this world.
they cannot.

a woman
is the ruler of her design.
a threatened man
cannot take that from her.
wear the suit..

Universe

it is not easy being the universe.
the burden of holding infinite weights.

the pressure of placing supernovae of struggles
on the shoulders of my sun.

wanting to hurt none,
yet sometimes hurting all,
and every second feels like the next could be
a starburst
of disbursed disarray.

but this Milky Way will not explode
while I am the queen of these cosmos.

totality on my back,
carrying it through my interstellar space.
celestial scenes and unforeseen dimensions
all depend on me to be.

it's not easy being the universe.
I have found my light in the sky
holding infinite weights

Face is a Portal

your face is a portal to me.
I see mountains of hope
where your cheeks rest.
words to change the world
run like rivers on your lips.
eyes that seek the saddened sights,
swooping them to sunshine.

I see mountains of peace
where your cheeks rest.
your ever-changing smile
pictures polaroid of better days.
met with eyes that seek the silver lining
among the pitfalls.
the dainty delights of life dance
on that button nose.

your ever-changing smile
shows me strength for all to come.
I kiss those cheeks
where hopeful mountains rest.
our future memories dance
on that button nose.
your face is a portal to me.

February

you were born under purple skies
with nobility boasting its wavelengths of color
through quartz impurities
that has all the power you need to hone here.

winter wandered in wonder
under the moon to which you were born,
bearing cups with water
that will overflow your world
with oceans of opportunity
for you to make a lasting mark.

auras of violet air pour through you
from the day you were born,
and fixed elements accentuate all those you touch
as you aim to become a visionary
among the masses of this world.

I saw inside you from the moment you were born,
under those skies in winter
when the force of your air took my breath away,
a most natural occurrence of substance
my eyes have ever seen.

I see you
for all that the constellation
to which you were formed under
will create among this world,
a light dawning in the age of the clarity
that lies within you.

within you, I see February forests still fruitful
and Amethysts that aid those who are sick
because that is what the universe gifted you
the day you were born.

and I, well, I get to be one speck
alongside the bright bursting alpha that is you.
I will float among your space,
and I will shimmer with you
in your atmosphere
as you carry the emotions
of those who will need your strength
amongst this piece of the everlasting sky.

but whatever you do,
you will radiate remarkable resilience,
and you will beam bravery
that sparkles with salvation.

I've known that since before you were born,
as my womb nurtured your spark
that would turn to glimmers that glow
across globes with your goodness.

and you, my darling, will always shine on.

Poetic Soul

I am a poetic soul
I have grown accustomed to triggering
sensitive emotions
by moving words around pages to express myself

my poetic soul
pushes my thoughts too far
and senses I ignored activate
when I try to understand myself

this poetic soul I live with
is a curse of recurring remembrance
and deep-rooted ridicule

I know no other way
than to try and convey how I got here
and what it sprouts in me

I am a poetic soul
who sprouts in all conditions
trying to make sense of these contents

growing through my pain
as I gain insight from this poetic soul
who knows my pen as a tool
to process the hurt through words
I convert into sensitive emotion

I have chosen the route
my poetic soul lays out for me
knowing it is not the easy road
but it is the only one I know how to travel

I cannot quit trying to express
what keeps me on this path
but I am not the one leading
I just follow

growing and staying whole
for my poetic soul

Reawakening

I reminisce in spring on my knees, elbows deep in dirt, turning the soil to sow memories into seeds that gives me another chance to start again. Sun not quite ready for me to bathe in, but just warm enough for me to feel its heat on the forehead that glistened for the first time since dormancy's chill took its shine away with all the other things it dulled and killed.

My sweat blends with the earth I have buried my hands into, and I remember. I am working through weeds, and composting twigs, and kneading clay from weathered rocks that I have kept my past under.

Year after year, I bruise my knees and lose my breath to wish away winter's wandering regrets into roots that I could rejuvenate new life into.

Restless reflections and recollections are taken with the wind that is stirring pollen and shifting the trees as they try to wake themselves. I could almost hear their sigh as they swayed awake. As I tuck time in topsoil, I sigh too.

I am trying to wake myself. I germinate my jaded yesterdays and mix it with the mulch to moisten the sprouts of sorrows that do not resonate with me anymore but deserve to be repurposed.

I reminisce in spring as I fertilize freshness over the remains of my remembrance, and I inhale its ever-changing shift on my lungs. The recency enters me, a foreign feeling that is familiar because each year it comes to me somehow.

It is different, the smell of spring. I welcome it as I exhale the dampened, darker days I have now turned into seeds that will grow to blooms in my garden like they do every year.

I wake myself as I remember all that was in winter, knowing what I have sown in spring will give me another chance to start again.

Cyclic and recurrent. Replanting recycled reminiscence, hoping I will wake before the frost comes again..

Holy Ground

There was a time when I needed to remind myself to breathe again. A moment when my brain forgot its job was to tell me to inhale, and I, well, I forgot what it felt like without air. It had been a long time since the discursive chatter of far too many perspectives scattered through my head, and in the chaos of conversing lips smacking like a fist to my face, I forgot to notice the rise and fall of my chest.

So, I ran against all logic through woods unknown to me. Red maple and white pine trees blended with the cottonwood I was stumbling around without a destination. I spotted stones with decaying creeping thyme that covered it, leading up a mountain I have never climbed but clambered my way up, gripping sycamore to hold me, knowing how bold it was of me not to pace myself on ascend.

Brooks babbled on either side as I climbed, and I could swear their talk was of me--the fool who ran without breath. But I needed to be far from the noise of others so that I could focus on my own. Huffing and puffing and panting and shuffling feet up steppingstones to what, I did not know.

I reached the top. Moss masked the soil I wished to sink my body into, bushes of ferns I could only wish to fall on. I listened for the rumble of my sigh that echoed amongst the beech and spruce that surrounded me. Slowly, I felt my diaphragm expand, taking small steps and focusing on my deep breath, surprised by what greeted me here. I am not a holy woman, and most times, I'm not sure what I believe at all. But raw wooden pews I chose to rest on showed me that I had been leading myself to church. A podium with the symbolism of devout practicing, reverent rows between dwarf willows that blow with the wind I can feel knock some sense into me.

I have never been here before, but I know a holy ground when I see one. I take in all the air as I stare at an emblem that has never resonated with me, but I see it more clearly than ever. Not for its association with religious sanctimony or high-praise ceremony, but for the infinite expansion it has brought to the planes I wish to breathe through again. I clasp my hands in a way I have not done since childhood, feeling them rise with my chest. Expanding me. Opening me. Sanctifying the lungs that have not had a chance to be my focus while I took to jetting through these woods.

I prayed, and I inhaled, and I thanked a God to which I'm unsure of for the blessing of the exhale I was given on top of sacred land. And the silence, oh, how the silence reigned through me while I reformed my heart back to its steady pace. I embrace the feeling that I am a mere visitor here, granted allowance to seek a haven in this place.

Coincidence does not exist in a world that led me to the only place I would have never sought for myself but needed, nonetheless.

Chestnut oak and huckleberry hugged me as I sat in this pew, taking in the slew of ventilation. I listened for the guide calls of the birds that flew over me, wingbeats in rhythm to the steady breath I found on this mountain, unexpectedly.

Climbing. Inhaling. Exhaling. Breathing in my new sanctuary.

I Am a Woman Who Knows

I am a woman who knows
no uncertainty can break me
for I am made of broken things

bullets engorge my back
where past lovers shot their rounds
yet I find new ways
to carry the baggage I'm left with
since I am a woman who knows

fractured ribs from those who kicked me
while I was down
still hold my body up just the same
for I am made of broken things

needles in my eye
where they tried to blind me
but I do not need my sight to see
because I am a woman who knows

shattered hearts still beat within their fragments
and mine has not grown cold despite betrayal
for I am made of broken things

cracks in my curves are proof that I have battled
I don't care if you can't see that I have won this war
for I am a woman who knows
and I am made of broken things.

About the Author

Christine Weimer is an award-winning writer and publisher from Queens, New York who is honing all the guts and glory of motherhood while promoting and supporting womxn writers through her independent press Our Galaxy Publishing as the Editor-in-Chief. She is the author of three poetry collections; *Tainted Lionheart*, which won the Gold Medal Poetry Award for *Readers' Favorite 2021*, *I Got to Know Nature*, and *Claiming the Throne*. Her most recent work is published in *The Order of Us* and *Venus Rising* anthologies and *Sunflower Station Press* literary magazine.

Visit Christine's official website and blog: **amindfulwriter.com**

Instagram: **@amindfulwriter**

A Three-Part Collection
by the Author

 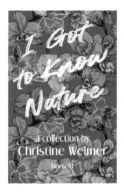 

OUR GALAXY
PUBLISHING

Our Galaxy Publishing serves women writers with the tools to unleash their creativity, amplify their voices, and publish their dreams.

We collaborate with aspiring authors and innovative creators to ensure their storytelling and publishing success with our expert, affordable services that provide the ultimate support between writer and provider. Our surefire resources accelerate women's influences and elevate their confidence to write and publish.

Our Galaxy is your personal story advocate. Come join our community.

Visit us on the web at: **ourgalaxypublishing.com**
Follow us on Instagram: **@ourgalaxypublishing**
Like us on Facebook: **ourgalaxyco**
Email us at: **ourgalaxypublishing@gmail.com**

CPSIA information can be obtained
at www.ICGtesting.com
Printed in the USA
BVHW091307061022
648825BV00013B/496